The King's Day

Louis XIV of France

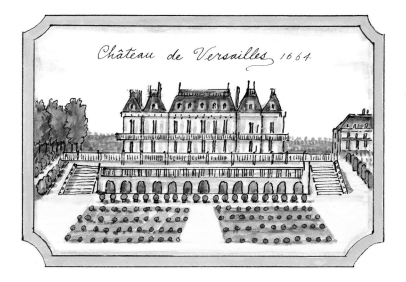

Château de Versailles 1664

by ALIKI

THOMAS Y. CROWELL   NEW YORK

The King's Day: Louis XIV of France   Copyright © 1989 by Aliki Brandenberg   Printed in the U.S.A.

Library of Congress Cataloging-in-Publication Data   Aliki. The King's day / written and illustrated by Aliki.
p.   cm.
Summary: A day in the life of France's King Louis XIV, focusing on the elaborate ceremonies which took
place when he dressed in the morning, ate his meals, conducted affairs of state, entertained, and finally,
when he prepared to go to bed at night.
ISBN 0-690-04588-3 : $ — ISBN 0-690-04590-5 (lib. bdg.) : $
1. Louis, XIV, King of France, 1638–1715—Juvenile literature.   2. France—Kings and rulers—Biography—
Juvenile literature.   3. France—Court and courtiers—History—17th century—Juvenile literature.
4. France—Social life and customs—17th–18th centuries—Juvenile literature.
[1. Louis XIV, King of France, 1638–1715.   2. Kings, queens, rulers, etc.   3. France—Social life
and customs—17th–18th centuries.]   I. Title.
DC129.A59 1989   944'.033'0924—dc19   [B]   [92]   88-38179   CIP   AC

1 2 3 4 5 6 7 8 9 10   First Edition

For Franz

ever patient in the Sun's long shadow

So glorious was Louis that he was called the "Sun King," and the sun became his symbol.

Louis XIV

was every inch a king.
He wore the curliest wigs,
the richest robes, the rarest jewels,
and the fanciest shoes in all of France.

Château des Tuileries

The Tuileries was one of the King's palaces in Paris, but Louis did not like city life. He preferred to live in the country.

Louis lived in glory

Fontainebleau was one of his many country residences. Its surrounding forest was a favorite royal hunting ground.

in many big palaces.

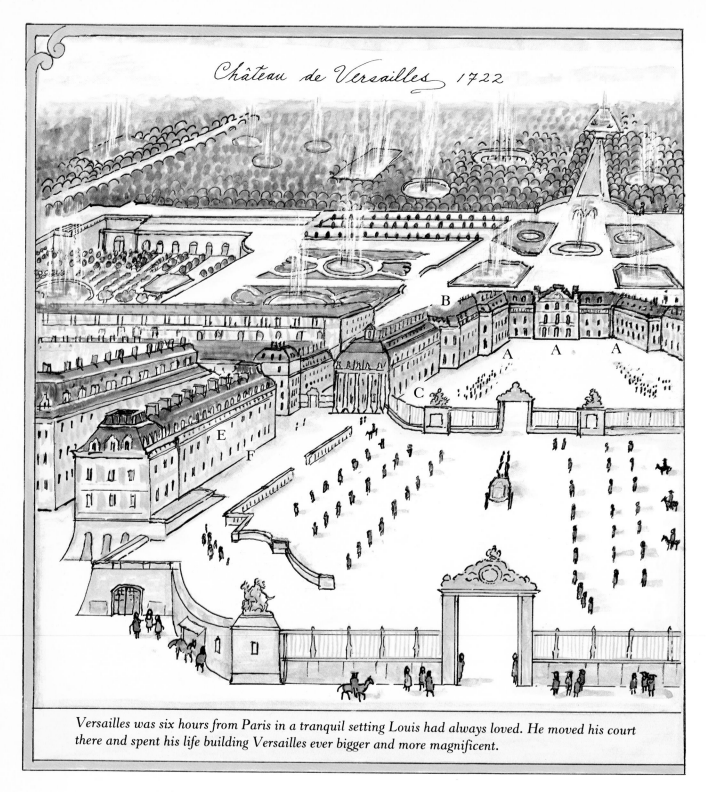

Château de Versailles 1722

Versailles was six hours from Paris in a tranquil setting Louis had always loved. He moved his court there and spent his life building Versailles ever bigger and more magnificent.

The biggest of all was the palace of Versailles.
Versailles was as spectacular as its King.

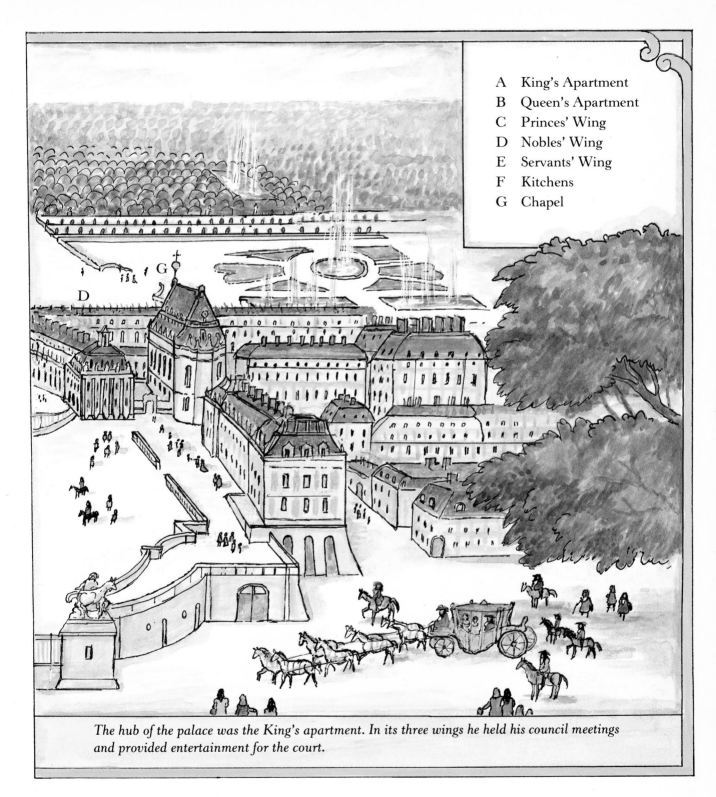

A King's Apartment
B Queen's Apartment
C Princes' Wing
D Nobles' Wing
E Servants' Wing
F Kitchens
G Chapel

The hub of the palace was the King's apartment. In its three wings he held his council meetings and provided entertainment for the court.

It was surrounded by endless gardens, parks, lakes, and fountains.

King
Louis XIV
(1638–1715)

Queen
Marie-Thérèse
(1638–1683)

Louis
The Dauphin
(Crown Prince)
(1661–1711)

*The King, his Queen, and their son, the **Dauphin**, heir to the throne. The Queen bore Louis six children, but only the **Dauphin** survived.*

It housed the King, his Queen, his mistresses,
all of his children, a swarm of relatives,

Louis
Comte
de
Vermandois

Louise de La Vallière
(1644–1710)

Marie
Anne
de
Bourbon

Louis
César
Comte
de
Vexin

Louise
Françoise

Louis
Auguste
Duc
de
Maine

Marquise de Montespan
(1641–1707)

Louise
Marie

Françoise
Marie

Louis
Alexandre
Comte
de
Toulouse

Madame de Maintenon
(1635–1719)

Two of the King's mistresses and the eight children they bore him.
Madame de Maintenon was the children's governess. Louis married her after the Queen died.

and ten thousand servants and courtiers who fought
for the honor of serving him.

And serve they did, for Louis's every move was an event.
Whether he was away—on a visit or on a battlefield—
  or at home in his palace, courtiers attended him.
They performed even the smallest task to win the King's favor,
  and followed him wherever he went.

Courtiers were noblemen who gave up the comfort of their own country estates to be at Versailles. For this honor, they lived in dark, cramped little rooms with their families and their own servants. The courtiers—and often their wives and other ladies of the court—were expected to attend all formal events. They had little time off for themselves, and had to eat between the King's meals. Louis liked it that way. They had no time to plot against him.

Preparations for the King's day began early
in the morning, before he woke.
There were no surprises, for Louis liked routine
as much as he liked ceremony.
His *Lever*—his getting-up ritual—was planned
in every detail, and the luckiest courtiers
were chosen to witness the whole affair.

Each favored courtier woke at dawn, dressed, and prepared for his long day. He would hover near the King, so Louis might toss him a favor—a free meal, a title, or an exemption from paying taxes. To get to the King's apartment for the **Lever,** *he made his way down dark staircases and through a maze of corridors and chambers.*

The King's Lever

The King slept—covers pulled down, windows open. He liked fresh air. At seven o'clock, the First **Valet de Chambre**, who slept in a corner of the royal bedchamber, folded up his own bed and prepared for the first big event of the day.

The Royal Faggot-Bearers lit the fire.

The Royal Watchmaker wound the royal clock.

The Royal Wigmaker brought in the King's dressing wig and morning wig. There were hundreds more in the royal wig room.

At the stroke of eight, the First **Valet** whispered, "Sire, it is time."

The King's Nurse rushed in to kiss him, just as she did every day of his life. The First Physician and First Surgeon followed, to give Louis the royal backrub and change the royal shirt—it was changed many times a day.

In the adjoining chamber, invited family and courtiers heard the news—the King was officially awake. They entered for the **Lever**. Only a chosen few of the men would assist, while Louis sipped his herb tea.

The King was wigged and robed.

He was shaved by the Royal Barber, and washed his own face with scented alcohol.

The Royal Chair-Carriers were honored to empty the royal chamberpot.

Dressing began with Louis discreetly shielded by his robe. First, a most favored courtier handed Louis his prewarmed lace shirt. Dressing continued with each separate garment, one by one.

*Finally, Louis was handed his handkerchief, his **Cordon Bleu**—the royal ribbon—and his sword, gloves, hat, and cane. Even on ordinary mornings, Louis wore embroidered clothes and shoes with diamond buckles.*

The King's *Lever* lasted two hours.
When it was finished, Louis was ready for his day.

At ten o'clock, he led a procession of the royal family and his entire court to chapel for mass.

This was one of the occasions during the day when someone might ask the King a favor. Though he was feared, Louis spoke kindly, listened patiently, and had perfect manners.

Louis was very pious. He prayed many times a day, and expected others to do the same with him. From the balcony in the chapel where he knelt, he could see if anyone was missing.

The King met with his few trusted ministers in the council chamber, next to his own bedchamber. He listened to their advice, and then he made his own decisions. Louis discussed his affairs with no one else—not even the **Dauphin** or his own brother, known as **Monsieur**.

At eleven o'clock he met with his council,
    and gave the orders of the day.
They discussed the progress of the kingdom—
    a new law, plans for a building,
    or the latest war.

Then it was time for the next big event—dinner—
    for the King's stomach was grumbling.

Throughout his reign, Louis tried to enlarge his kingdom, and often made war with France's neighbors. He followed his army abroad, and commanded his troops until the battle was over.

The King had dinner—his *Petit Couvert*—at one o'clock.
When he dined in private, he ate alone—
    but he was never really alone.
Servants, and perhaps a guest or two,
    stood around and waited and watched.

*Not even the **Dauphin** was offered a seat in the King's bedchamber when Louis dined, and ladies were never invited.*

*Before every meal, each dish was tasted by the **Maître d'Hôtel** and the **Officer of the Kitchen**, to make sure it was safe for the King to eat, and tasty enough.*

Louis loved to eat.
He had an enormous appetite,
   and satisfied it well.
It took five hundred servants to prepare his meals,
   and Louis kept them busy.

Even though forks had been invented, the King always ate with his fingers, wiping them on a damp napkin before and after.

Although it didn't show, doctors would discover, after his death, that Louis's stomach was twice the size of an ordinary one. This accounted for his enormous appetite.

Sometimes he dined *au public*.

Then any respectable person could journey to Versailles,
  file past the King, and see the spectacle for himself.

Anyone who saw the King's dinner being carried in the halls had to bow to it.

The menu might be four soups, a stuffed pheasant,
   a partridge, a duck, some mutton, sliced ham, three salads,
   boiled eggs, a dish of pastry, fruit, and compotes.
He ate all of it, and washed it down with diluted wine.

The kitchens were so far away, the food arrived cold—but there was enough of it.

Louis was an outdoor man.
Every afternoon he changed his clothes and wig
   and went out into the fresh air—rain or shine.
He went hunting or shooting or riding.

Louis loved to hunt, and he loved his five hundred dogs, too. He kept many of them in gilded kennels in a chamber near his own and fed them himself, morning and night.

He took outings in the countryside,

Louis invited the ladies of the court to ride with him, and offered them food on the way. Louis never ate between meals but he liked to see others eat, even if he didn't join them.

or strolled in the gardens of Versailles.
It was his favorite time of day.

Louis loved flowers. In his gardens, he had four million tulips, and two thousand orange trees planted in silver tubs. Everyone admired the beautiful gardens, but dreaded having to walk in them—they were so vast.

Appartement *was held three times a week from seven to ten o'clock in the King's apartment. The many chambers glowed with candlelight. Louis strode among his courtiers in his diamond-studded clothes, chatting, listening, and noticing everything.*

After a rest, Louis dressed for *Appartement*—
   an "open house" he held for his court.
They heard a concert, watched a play or a dance,
   had refreshments, and played games.
Like it or not, everyone was expected to attend,
   for Louis wanted to know where everyone was.
He never forgot that all of France belonged to him.
Louis XIV was in control.

Ballet was performed in lavish productions at Louis's court. All of the dancers were men. When he was young, Louis danced too.

France's greatest playwrights and composers wrote plays and operas for **Appartement**.

Cards and billiards were favorite games of the court. When the King played billiards, everyone watched.

Then, when everyone else was nodding with sleep,
    Louis had supper.
The royal family ate with him at the *Grand Couvert*,
    while the court looked on.
The *Grand Couvert* was even more excessive
    than the *Petit Couvert*.
This time, there were some forty dishes served.
No wonder Louis never ate between meals.

The **Grand Couvert** was dull and unbearably quiet. The King did not like to talk while he ate, nor to listen, either.

When Louis reached his bedchamber at last,
 he still was not alone.
It was time for the final event of the day—
 the *Coucher*—his going-to-bed ceremony.

The ladies of the court bid Louis good night and went off to their beds.

The royal family followed for a chat and a good-night. When they left, Louis went to feed his dogs and returned for the **Coucher**.

*The **Coucher** was a repeat of the **Lever**, but in reverse. The greatest honor of the day was to hold the candle that lit the ceremony.*

By one-thirty AM, the King was finally in his nightshirt,
   his nightcap, and his bed,
      and his weary courtiers were free to trudge up to theirs.

The dawn of a new day was only a few hours away.

The King's day was repeated again and again,
for Louis was King a long seventy-two years.
He was a brilliant ruler who controlled the rich and poor,
noble and peasant, with absolute power. He knew just what
he wanted for his kingdom, and brought spectacular glory
to it and to the seventeenth century in which he lived.
Louis XIV of France was a born King.

Chronology of King Louis XIV

1638   Louis was born on September 5.

1643   Louis became King when his father, Louis XIII, died.

1660   Louis married Marie-Thérèse of Spain.

1661   Louis assumed full power when his prime minister died.

1662   Building of Versailles began.

1682   Louis moved his court to Versailles.

1683   Queen Marie-Thérèse died, aged 48.

1684   Louis married Madame de Maintenon.

1711   Louis's son and heir, the Dauphin, died, aged 50.

1715   Louis died, aged 77.

1715   Louis XIV was succeeded by his great-grandson, Louis XV, aged 5.

Definitions of French words

Appartement	The King's "open house," which took place in his apartment	*Grand Couvert*	Supper
Au public	In public	*Lever*	Getting-up ceremony
Château	Gentleman's residence	*Maître d'Hôtel*	House steward
Cordon Bleu	Blue ribbon indicating royalty	*Monsieur*	Sir
Coucher	Going-to-bed ceremony	*Petit Couvert*	Dinner
Dauphin	Crown prince, heir to the throne	*Valet de Chambre*	Servant of the bedchamber